A special thank-you for

Lila (baby sis)

You are special to me.
Thank you for being my sister.

With love and gratitude,

Lorrie (old sis)

Date

12 - 25 - 03

the thank you series™

$\mathcal{O}$ur purpose at Howard Publishing is to:
- *Increase faith* in the hearts of growing Christians
- *Inspire holiness* in the lives of believers
- *Instill hope* in the hearts of struggling people everywhere

Because He's coming again!

Thank You Sister © 2002 by Howard Publishing Company
All rights reserved. Printed in the United States of America

Published by Howard Publishing Co., Inc.
3117 North 7th Street, West Monroe, Louisiana 71291-2227

02 03 04 05 06 07 08 09 10 11   10 9 8 7 6 5 4 3 2 1

Stories by Debbie Webb
Edited by Between the Lines
Interior design by LinDee Loveland and Stephanie Denney

ISBN: 1-58229-274-4

thank you *sister*

a collection of poems,
prayers, stories, quotes, and
scriptures to say thank you

HOWARD
PUBLISHING CO.

sister

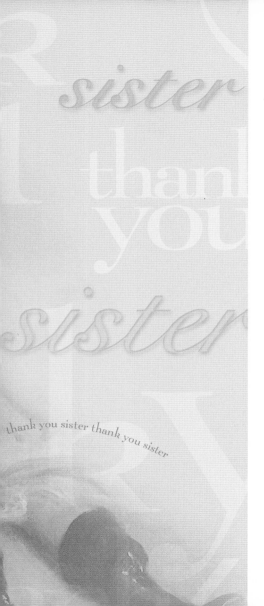

thank
you

Thank you for

allowing me to

feel that I can be

who I really am

and still be loved

by you.

thank
you

sister

Dear *Lila*,

If it had been possible to choose a woman with whom I would share my history, my heritage, and my heart; a woman I would trust with my deepest secrets, my greatest fears, my highest hopes; a friend, a confidante, a companion, and encourager; a woman to call my sister; I would have chosen you.

My heart is filled with the memories of special times only sisters can share. You have been my playmate, fashion consultant, counselor, and faithful friend. You've forgiven me when I didn't deserve it, applauded me when I succeeded, believed in me even when I faltered, comforted me when I cried, and stuck with me through thick and thin.

Now that we're grown, I want to tell you how I feel—how I've always felt—about having you for a sister. I hope that in the words of this little book you'll find my affection, admiration, and appreciation.

Love,

Larrie

Before I ever saw myself, I saw my sister. When I was still too small for mirrors, I saw her as the reflection that proved my own existence.

DANZY SENNA

For there is no friend like a sister
In calm or stormy weather;
To cheer one on the tedious way,
To fetch one if one goes astray,
To lift one if one totters down,
To strengthen whilst one stands.

—*Christina Rossetti*

Miss Searcy High

Becky couldn't believe this was happening. Today Miss Searcy High would be announced, and she was one of five finalists. She felt both anticipation and hopelessness. She knew she wouldn't have a chance against her sister Jenny.

Jenny had been homecoming queen, White County Fair queen, and club sweetheart. She was head cheerleader and the most sought-after girl at school. Jenny was beautiful, inside and out. Long, silky, blonde hair fell gracefully onto her shoulders and cascaded down her back. Her creamy complexion served as the canvas upon which her blazing brown eyes sparkled and shimmered. A dazzling row of perfect ivory graced her radiant smile, accompanied by a pair of lush lips tinted with a hint of rose. She was drop-dead gorgeous—no doubt about it.

Next to Jenny, Becky felt positively common. Her naturally curly, brunette hair, though intriguing, was untamable. A slight overbite made her smile jump out at you before the rest of her face, and her eyes, though large and luminous, were usually distracted—lost somewhere deep in thought. Becky loved her sister, but she had always secretly wished that she *were* her sister!

Jenny was always encouraging Becky to join her in beauty pageants, to try out for the drill team or the cheerleading squad. "Come on, Becky, you'll do great. You're so beautiful and so talented. I just know you'll make it."

But Becky had always shied away from such contests, focusing on more intellectual pursuits. Academia was more suited to her taste than beauty pageants and dance routines. Still, Becky felt that she never really fit in because she didn't have Jenny's glamour or popularity. She was sure she was doomed to be nothing more in life than Jenny Dempsey's little sister.

Then, just this week, Becky learned that she had been nominated for Miss Searcy High. The shock had sent her thoughts reeling as she wandered, dazed, from the principal's office where

Miss Searcy High

she'd received the news. *But what about Jenny? I can't be nominated if Jenny isn't.* Caught between exhilaration and anxiety, Becky had struggled unsuccessfully to concentrate in her morning classes.

That noon Becky ran to the parking lot to catch her sister on her way off-campus for lunch.

"Hey, Jenny!" she shouted breathlessly. "Wait up!"

"What is it, Beck?" Jenny shouted back as she started toward her sister.

"Were you nominated for Miss Searcy High?" Becky asked as she met her sister.

"As a matter of fact, I was! How did you know?"

"Because you always are Jenny, can you believe I was, too?" Becky squealed.

"Yes!" Jenny squealed back, smiling and taking hold of her little sister's hands. "As a matter of fact, I wouldn't have believed it if you *weren't* nominated. It's good to know this student body has *some* good judgment *some* of the time. Congratulations!"

"Oh, Jen," Becky suddenly sobered. "I don't want to *win*. I know you should get it. But I just couldn't believe that I was even nominated. For me, that's just as good as winning!"

Jenny squeezed her sister's hands and rubbed them between hers affectionately. "No, Beck, *you* should win. If these matters were judged by what's in the heart, it would be a done deal!"

The week had seemed to drag on forever as Becky awaited the day of the announcement. Her words to Jenny about her nomination being just as good as winning had worn thin before the first day was done. Becky wanted that title. And she felt guilty for wanting to win over her sister. Why was she even setting herself up for this kind of disappointment? She didn't have a chance, and she knew it.

Throughout the week, tension had mounted. Becky began to suspect everything Jenny did as a political maneuver—the clothes she wore, the people she hung out with, and the teachers she talked to. Becky hated these feelings. Jenny had always been her best friend, never her rival.

Now, as she stared absently out the second-story classroom window at students moving along the sidewalk, a familiar figure caught her eye. She recognized Jenny's fast gait from their childhood days—it was her version of concealed excitement. *Why wouldn't she be excited?* Becky thought. *She knows she's going to win. I just wish I could be as happy as she is.*

Miss Searcy High

❧

Jenny *was* excited. She had been nervous all week too—but she wasn't worried about losing; she was worried that she might win. She genuinely wanted Becky to finally be recognized for the talented, outstanding person Jenny knew her to be.

Then, this morning Jenny had been called to the office. Mrs. Ruskin, the principal, advised her privately that she had won the title. The announcement would be made over the intercom at lunch that day. Jenny sat stunned and silent.

Mrs. Ruskin noticed her subdued reaction. "Jenny, what's the matter? I thought you'd be elated. This is an honor! Is there a problem?"

Jenny felt miserable. "Mrs. Ruskin, I am honored, and I don't mean to appear otherwise. But my sister was nominated too, and she's never won anything like this. I just really wanted her to win." Her voice wavered with emotion.

Mrs. Ruskin didn't know what to say. She was touched by the gracious heart of this young woman, but the votes had been cast.

Suddenly, Jenny's eyes lit up. "Mrs. Ruskin, who was the runner-up?"

Mrs. Ruskin's brow furrowed into a frown. "That's confidential, Jenny. I really can't say."

"Please try to understand," Jenny persisted. "If I knew Becky was the runner-up, I would decline the title and it could go to her—right?"

"Well, I suppose so, but I still can't reveal who is the runner-up." Mrs. Ruskin shifted uncomfortably in her seat. She had always adhered strictly to the contest guidelines, but the sacrificial love of this sister made bending the rules tempting.

"I've got it!" Jenny snapped her fingers as the idea came to her. "I'll decline the title with a contingency: If Becky's the runner-up, then I refuse to accept. If not, I'll never say another word. How's that?" Jenny arched her eyebrows in hope.

"OK, Jenny," Mrs. Ruskin conceded with a barely concealed smile. "I accept your contingent forfeit of the title. The new Miss Searcy High will be announced at noon," she said, trying to make everything as official as possible.

"So, it's Becky?" Jenny asked.

"You'll have to wait until lunch, just like everyone else," Mrs. Ruskin answered in mock seriousness. Jenny grinned her thanks and headed out of the office.

Miss Searcy High

 *sister*

After her secret meeting, she practically floated down the sidewalk and up the stairs to the main building, looking as though she were on top of the world.

Lunchtime finally came, and the two sisters met each other at an agreed-upon spot in the cafeteria. Becky seemed quiet and pensive. She couldn't remember ever feeling so vulnerable. She couldn't even look Jenny in the eye because she wasn't accustomed to the strange feelings of competition she felt toward her sister. Jenny was bubbly and full of anticipation.

"Students, please be seated for a special announcement!" The voice came blaring over the intercom. Becky's eyes darted around the room uncomfortably. She spotted the nearest exit and planned her escape. Why hadn't she just stayed home today and spared herself the agony and humiliation?

"It is our pleasure to announce the winner for the title of Miss Searcy High this year..."

Just get it over with, please, Becky thought. Jenny reached under the table and grabbed her hand, holding on hard. *Why are you so anxious?* Becky wondered in response to her gesture. *You know you're the winner.*

The intercom crackled again, and the voice blared: "Please join me in congratulating...Becky Dempsey—Miss Searcy High!"

Cheers, whistles, applause! The air was filled with noise. Jenny grabbed Becky's face in her hands and shouted above the noise, "Did you hear that, Beck, you *won!*"

"Jenny," Becky stammered, taken aback, "it should have been you. I'm so sorry." Her feelings of competition melted into genuine disappointment for her sister.

"No, Beck," Jenny said, wrapping her up in a big hug, "it should be you!"

Becky was overwhelmed by the friendship, love, and support Jenny showed at her victory and returned the hug with great affection. Then she squeezed Jenny's hand one last time before walking to the stage to accept her title. The new Miss Searcy High sent out her thanks in an unreserved, radiant smile. Looking out over the sea of faces whose approval she had sought, Becky's eyes locked with Jenny's. Becky instantly realized that Jenny's approval was the only one that really mattered.

Miss Searcy High

sister

thank you

Sister, you've always

been a playmate, a

fashion consultant,

a champion,

a counselor, an

advocate, and a

faithful friend.

a blessing
for you

*M*ay the bond we share as sisters

*B*ring you peace when days get long.

*M*ay the love you hear in my voice

*B*e a warm and soothing song.

sister

May the mem'ries of our childhood

Fill your heart with strength and love.

May God's promise of the future

Bring warm assurance from above.

sister thank you sister thank you sister thank you sister thank you sister thank you sister thank you sister thank you sister thank you sister thank you sister thank you sister thank you sister thank you sister thank you sister thank you sister thank you sister thank you sister thank you sister thank you sister thank you sister

What greater thing is there for human souls than to feel that they are joined for life— to be with each other in silent unspeakable memories.

GEORGE ELIOT

sister

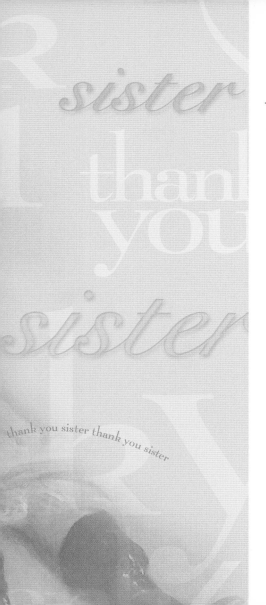

thank
you

Thank you for

defending me

when I couldn't

stand up for

myself.

Yet still my fate permits me this relief,
To write to lovely Delia all my grief.
To you alone I venture to complain;
From others hourly strive to hide my pain.

—*Abigail Colman Dennie*
Lines from a letter to her sister,
poet Jane Colman Turrell

A ministering
angel shall
my sister be.

WILLIAM SHAKESPEARE

The Perfect Doll

Tracie had always hated the dark. It had a thickness about it that clogged her head and made rational thought difficult. She strained to get her bearings; but out here in this blackness, there was no way.

Yet the circumstances at hand demanded clear thinking. Her sister Bailey lay unconscious on the pavement. Tracie could just make out the dark circle of blood forming under Bailey's head. She had been thrown through the windshield as her car careened off the road and over the embankment just minutes before.

Think, Tracie—try to think... If she didn't find a way to stop the hemorrhaging soon, she felt certain Bailey would bleed to death. But she felt faint, dizzy, unable to concentrate.

I think I could stop the bleeding if I had a bandage of some sort. Remembering her CPR training from last summer, she ripped her left sleeve off her blouse. *I just wish it weren't so dark.* Feeling for the warm, wet spot on the back of Bailey's head, Tracie wrapped and tied the piece of cloth as tightly as she dared.

Tracie and Bailey had been on their way home from Auburn University for the holidays. They were several hours into the trip and had spent most of the time talking about people and events at school. About thirty minutes earlier, their conversation had turned toward home.

Her mind drifted again... Bailey had been reminiscing about the Christmas when she was seven and Tracie was nine. They had gotten new dolls, as they did every Christmas. Their mother always matched the appearance of the dolls as closely as possible to that of the girls—one brunette, the other blonde.

That year, brunette Bailey accidentally opened the wrong package and immediately fell in love with the blonde-haired doll. Tracie was left with the dark-haired doll.

Tracie really wanted that blonde baby. She tried to stay composed, but she was seething. Bailey had been so excited over her own good fortune that she didn't notice her sister's reaction...

The Perfect Doll

I really need some light. Tracie shifted. She winced at the sharp pain that shot through her thigh, but she was sure her nausea and lightheadedness were caused by the disorienting darkness. She cradled her sister's head, talking softly to her— talking about the dolls. Bailey loved to relive the doll story. Every time Tracie thought about it, she cringed...

Tracie's first attempt at obtaining the blonde doll was overt. She simply said, "Mom, why did you give Bailey my doll?"

"I guess the boxes got mixed up when I wrapped them, Honey. But it wasn't really yours until you opened it, so this one is yours after all!"

That was nonsense to Tracie. The blonde doll was *always* hers! Later that day she sneaked into the bedroom where the dolls lay in their cradles and switched them—including their outfits, to make it as subtle as possible.

When Bailey went to get her doll, everyone in the house heard her scream. She accused her older brother and solicited Tracie's help getting the dolls back into their proper outfits. Then, to Tracie's chagrin, Bailey vowed never to take her eyes off her doll again...

It's so cold! Tracie shivered and held her hand over Bailey's mouth. She was still breathing, but it seemed weak and shallow. "Hang on, Bailey," she whispered...

Next, Tracie had suggested bathing the dolls. After washing and rinsing them, she sent Bailey to lay towels on the bed for the wet babies. As soon as Bailey stepped out of the bathroom, Tracie shut the door quietly behind her and locked it.

With her mother's tweezers, Tracie yanked locks of hair out of the blonde doll's scalp, leaving gaping bald spots. She put the hair in the tub so it would appear to have fallen out during the washing.

When Bailey returned, the floating hair immediately caught her attention. "Tracie!" she screamed. "My baby's hair is falling out!"

"Oh, no," Tracie responded, acting sorry for her sister. "I'll trade dolls if you want."

"No," Bailey said with tears in her eyes. "I love her even with bald spots. How would you feel if Mama gave you away just because you weren't perfect..."

Bailey, please don't die, Tracie pleaded silently. She was so weak that words wouldn't come anymore. Tracie lay down next to her sister, holding her head in the crook of her arm to keep pressure on the wound. Tears stung her eyes. She kissed her sister's forehead and fell into a semiconscious state...

The Perfect Doll

Finally, Tracie had tried a little psychology. "Bailey, do you really like your doll?"

"Yes! I love her!" Bailey exclaimed. "Don't you?"

"Well, I'm getting a little old to play with dolls, but I feel sorry that I got the best one when you're the one who will play with yours the most."

"You really think yours is best?" Bailey asked uncertainly.

"Of course! Everyone does!" Tracie fibbed.

Bailey's face fell with her heart. She had been certain her doll was the most beautiful, but now she felt unsure. "I didn't know you thought you were too old to play with dolls," she said sadly. Then the pieces began to fall into place in her young mind.

"You aren't really too old to play with dolls. You just want my doll, don't you?"

Tracie was caught. "Yes. I *always* get the blonde babies!"

Bailey looked up at her sister with both hurt and love in her eyes. "You can have her, Tracie. You should have just told me. I'd have given her to you if I'd known."

Bailey relinquished the doll with total abandon. She never looked back, and the sisters played together with them for years afterward. Tracie had suffered a silent guilt for years.

❧

Bailey awoke in a hospital room. Her mother's face was the first thing she saw. "Where's Tracie?" she asked groggily.

"She's in the next bed, Honey," her mother whispered. "She's still sleeping."

"What happened?" The last thing she remembered was laughing about Tracie and that silly doll.

Her mother told her about the accident. "You would have died, but your sister saved your life."

Bailey's eyes grew wide and teary. "Is she OK?"

"She'll be fine. A major artery in her thigh was punctured, and she almost bled to death. She was so busy tending to you, she didn't even know she was hurt."

"Oh, Mom," Bailey sobbed, "I love her so much. What would I do without her?"

"The love between sisters is a powerful thing, Bailey, and Tracie does love you—even more than you knew," her mother consoled. "And now you both know never to take that for granted."

Tracie awoke at the sound of their voices. Relieved to hear Bailey, Tracie roused herself just enough to say, "Hey, sister— wanna play dolls?"

The Perfect Doll

thank you sister thank you sister thank you sister thank you sister thank you sister

sister

thank
you

It's comforting

to know I have

someone who

shares the same

past and who

will be part of

my life forever.

1 Thessalonians
1:3

NIV

[I] CONTINUALLY REMEMBER BEFORE OUR GOD AND FATHER YOUR WORK PRODUCED BY FAITH, YOUR LABOR PROMPTED BY LOVE, AND YOUR ENDURANCE INSPIRED BY HOPE.

My sister! With that thrilling word
Let thoughts unnumbered wildly spring!
What echoes in my heart are stirred
While thus I touch the trembling string.

—*Margaret Davidson*

sister

thank you

It's nice to know

there's someone in

the world whom I

can trust with all

my heart.

thank **you**

sister

Dear Heavenly Father,

I'm certain You handpicked my sister—that in Your eternal wisdom and generous heart, You planned the wonderful ways she would enrich my life. I've felt Your tender touch through her hands. I've experienced Your great love through her heart. I've seen Your genuine concern in her eyes. And I've known Your faithfulness through her devotion.

Thank You, Lord, for her insight and wisdom, her intuitive understanding, her contagious joy, and her constant encouragement. Thank You for her tender care and her stubborn insistence on what's best for me. Thank You for the memories we've shared, the legacy we've inherited, and the bond that has only strengthened over the years.

Father, I ask that Your blessing would be poured out generously on her life. Return to her the tremendous joy she has given me by being my sister.

Amen.

In thee my
soul shall own
combined,
the sister and
the friend.

CATHERINE KILLIGREW